BASKETBALL STARS

**ADAM
ELLIOTT
SEGAL**

FIREFLY BOOKS

A FIREFLY BOOK

Published by Firefly Books Ltd. 2017

First printing

Publisher Cataloging-in-Publication Data (U.S.)
Names: Segal, Adam Elliott, author.
Title: Basketball Stars / Adam Elliott Segal.
Description: Richmond Hill, Ontario, Canada : Firefly Books, 2017. | Summary: Biographies of some
    of basketball's best players as defined by their skills and the character traits that make them
    successful.
Identifiers: ISBN 978-1-77085-827-5 (hardcover) | 978-1-77085-772-8 (paperback)
Subjects: LCSH: Basketball players – Biography -- Juvenile literature. | Basketball – Biography –
    Juvenile literature. | BISAC: JUVENILE NONFICTION / Biography & Autobiography / Sports &
    Recreation. | JUVENILE NONFICTION / Sports & Recreation / Basketball.
Classification: LCC GV884.A1S443 |DDC 796.3230922 – dc23

Library and Archives Canada Cataloguing in Publication
Segal, Adam Elliott, author
        Basketball stars / Adam Elliott Segal.
ISBN 978-1-77085-827-5 (hardcover).--ISBN 978-1-77085-772-8 (softcover)
        1. Basketball players--United States--Biography--Juvenile literature.
2. National Basketball Association--Biography--Juvenile literature.
3. National Basketball Association--Juvenile literature. I. Title.
GV884.A1S45 2017   j796.323092'273   C2017-902104-4

Published in the United States by
Firefly Books (U.S.) Inc.
P.O. Box 1338, Ellicott Station
Buffalo, New York 14205

Published in Canada by
Firefly Books Ltd.
50 Staples Avenue, Unit 1
Richmond Hill, Ontario L4B 0A7

Cover and interior design: Kimberley Young

Printed in China

Canada We acknowledge the financial support of the Government of Canada.

Table of Contents

Basketball Basics ④

Player Profiles ⑱

Photo Credits ⑭

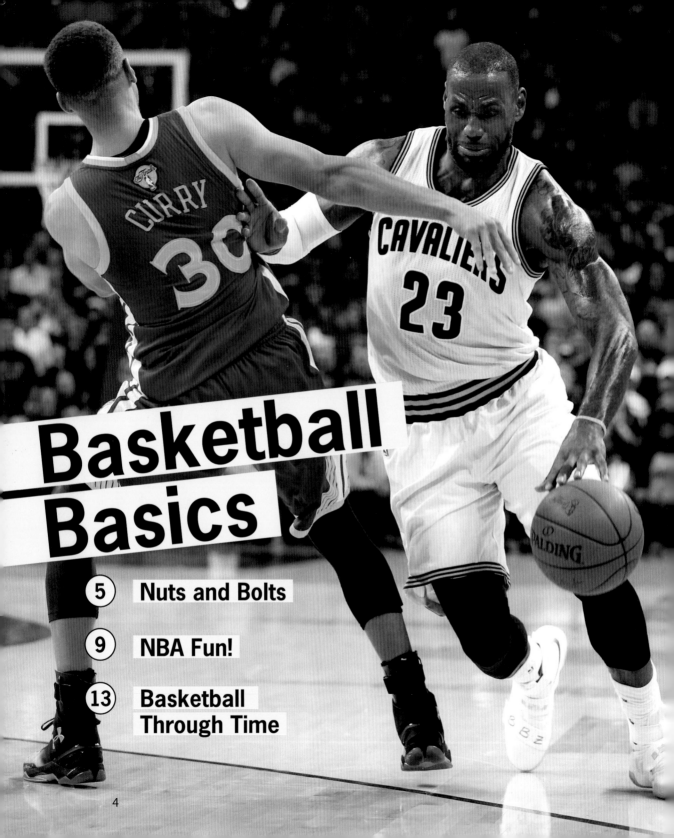

Basketball
Basics

5   **Nuts and Bolts**

9   **NBA Fun!**

13   **Basketball Through Time**

NUTS AND BOLTS

IT'S ALL ABOUT POSITION

You probably already know the positions — center, forward and guard. But did you know that each position is assigned a number?

1 **POINT GUARD, AKA "THE ONE"**
Typically the shortest and quickest player on the team, the point guard has two main assets: dribbling and passing. "The one" often runs set plays from the top of the three-point line.

2 **SHOOTING GUARD, AKA "THE TWO"**
"The two" is a little bigger than the point guard, typically has a stronger, more consistent shot and is a solid defender. Sometimes the shooting guard is referred to as the two guard.

3 **SMALL FORWARD, AKA "THE THREE"**
A small forward has a good post game, quickness and an ability to put the ball on the floor 1-on-1. "The three" can often shift positions, playing big against a shooting guard or small against a power forward.

4 **POWER FORWARD, AKA "THE FOUR"**
The power forward is a rebounder, an inside presence and a big body around the basket. "The four" hustles big time and makes life difficult for the opposing defense.

5 **CENTER, AKA "THE FIVE"**
"The five" is the biggest player on the court (sometimes measuring seven-feet tall) and the post-up man in the middle. Although not the quickest player, the center's size makes up for this lack of speed, and "the five" is typically a dunking machine.

THE BALL

What's a basketball made of? Why leather, of course! Look a little closer and you'll notice the manufacturer's name, Spalding, lasered on the front of every official NBA ball. Each ball is between 29½ and 30 inches (75–76 cm) in circumference and weighs between 20 and 22 ounces (567–624 g). It should be inflated to between 7 and 9 psi.

TIME

GAME TIME – 48 minutes split into four 12-minute quarters with a 15-minute halftime.

SHOT CLOCK – The maximum time for each possession is 24 seconds.

SEASON – 82 games in an NBA regular season.

THE EVOLUTION OF THE KEY

Did you know the free-throw lane, or "key," used to look like a keyhole? That's where it got its nickname! The NBA key has changed over the history of the league to make it more challenging for players to dominate the area closest to the basket.

1946–1950
6 ft (1.8 m) wide

1951–1963
12 ft (3.7 m) wide

1964–present
16 ft (4.9 m) wide

Points

How is basketball scored? It's pretty simple!

1 Each free throw you make is worth one point. If you make both, it's as good as making a basket! If you are fouled while taking a three-pointer, you can take three tries at the line.

2 Every basket inside the three-point line counts as two points. It doesn't matter if it's a slam dunk or a step-back jump shot!

3 Known as a "trey," "from downtown," "from three-point land" and "beyond the arc," any shot taken from beyond the three-point line scores three points.

4 There's only one way to score four points at once: if you are fouled in the act of shooting a three and still make the shot, you're awarded a free throw. If you make it — bam! It's a four-point play!

SIDELINE

BASELINE

FREE-THROW LINE

THREE-POINT LINE

SIDELINE

LEARN THE LINGO

Basketball has a language of its own! Here are some terms you might hear next time you watch a game.

BOARD – Another word for a rebound.

DIME – Another word for an assist.

DOUBLE-DOUBLE – Recording double-digit stats in any two of five categories (points, assists, rebounds, steals and blocks) in one game.

FIELD GOAL – Any shot attempt by a player, not counting free throws.

PERIMETER – The area on the court outside the key but inside the three-point line.

POST UP – When an offensive player is positioned near the basket with his or her back to the basket. In this position, the player can protect the ball from a defender and easily receive passes from a teammate.

TRIPLE-DOUBLE – Recording double-digit stats in any three of five categories (points, assists, rebounds, steals and blocks) in one game.

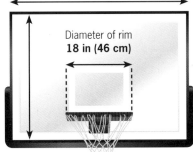

Width of backboard
6 ft (1.8 m)

Diameter of rim
18 in (46 cm)

Height of backboard
3 ft 6 in (1.1 m)

Diameter of ball
9 in (23 cm)

Width of court
50 ft (15.2 m)

Height of basket
10 ft (3 m)

Width of key **16 ft (4.9 m)**

Length of half-court **47 ft (14.3 m)**

Length of court **94 ft (28.7 m)**

The Court

Most Common Violations

Over and back – Once you bring the ball over the centerline, you can't bring it back. If you do, the other team gets the ball.

Double dribble – Did you know you can only legally dribble the ball with one hand? If you use both hands or interrupt a dribble by holding the ball, it's called a double dribble.

Three-second rule or "three in the key" – You get just three seconds to stay put in the offensive free-throw lane, also known as "the key." If you spend more than three seconds in that space, the other team is awarded the ball.

24-second shot clock violation – If a team doesn't attempt a shot (that hits the rim) within 24 seconds, it loses possession of the ball.

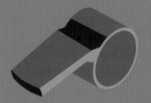

OFFICIALS

There are three referees on the court at a time, and one is designated the crew chief. Other people on the officiating team include the timekeeper and the official scorer. Currently, Lauren Holtkamp is the NBA's only female ref.

Goaltending – If a player interferes with a shot that is on a downward path to the hoop or a ball that is on the rim, the shot is considered in and the offensive team gets the basket.

Traveling – If you take three or more steps without dribbling the ball, you have traveled and your team loses the ball.

Fouls

Defensive foul – Defensive players are issued a foul when they make contact with an opponent. If the opponent is shooting when he or she is fouled, the opponent receives two or three free throws, depending on whether it was a two-pointer or a three-pointer.

Offensive foul – When an offensive player runs into a defender who has both feet planted on the court, that's called charging. He or she is given one personal foul.

Technical foul – Technical fouls are usually given to players for unsportsmanlike conduct. Nicknames for these fouls include "T'ed up" and "tech." Did you know even coaches can be T'ed up?

The tallest player in the NBA history was **MANUTE BOL** at 7-foot-7. He and Muggsy Bogues, the NBA's shortest player, even played together for the Washington Bullets during the 1987–88 season.

7' 7"

6' 7"

5' 7"

The average player is 6-foot-7.

The smallest player in NBA history is **MUGGSY BOGUES**, who tops out at 5-foot-3. He could even dunk!

The shortest player to win the slam dunk contest is **SPUD WEBB**, who won in 1986. He is only 5-foot-7!

All-Around Athletes

Some interesting athletes have been drafted into the NBA, including former gold-medal-winning sprinter **CARL LEWIS** (10th round pick by the Chicago Bulls in 1984) and Hall of Fame baseball player **DAVE WINFIELD** (5th round pick by the Atlanta Hawks in 1973).

9

Jersey Foul

Wondering what the ugliest jerseys in NBA history are? Have a look at these jersey fouls.

Denver Nuggets jersey ca. 1980s–90s

Toronto Raptors jersey ca. 1990s

Vancouver Grizzlies jersey ca. 1990s

Quiz Time!

4. What year did the three-point line get introduced?
   a) 1945
   b) 1967
   c) 1979
   d) 1989

1. Who holds the record for the most points in an NBA game?
   a) Wilt Chamberlain
   b) Kobe Bryant
   c) Michael Jordan
   d) Uncle Drew

5. Before the Washington Wizards became the Wizards, what were they called?
   a) Washington Weezils
   b) Washington Warriors
   c) Washington Bullets
   d) Washington Weenies

2. Who holds the record for the most rebounds in an NBA game?
   a) Bill Russell
   b) Wilt Chamberlain
   c) Shaquille O'Neal
   d) Charles Barkley

3. Who was the oldest player during the 2016–17 season?
   a) Kevin Garnett
   b) Andre Miller
   c) Paul Pierce
   d) Vince Carter

4. c) 1979
The first basket from "downtown" is credited to Chris Ford, a Boston Celtics guard who hit the deep shot on October 12, 1979. George Mikan of the American Basketball Association instituted the three-point line during the 1967–68 ABA season, and a decade later, the rule was adopted by the NBA.

5. c) Washington Bullets
The Washington Wizards were called the Bullets from 1974 to 1997. For the franchise's first season in the nation's capital in 1972–73, they were called the Capital Bullets.

1. a) Wilt Chamberlain
On March 2, 1962, Chamberlain scored 100 points against the New York Knicks as a member of the Philadelphia Warriors. The final score was 169–147 for the Warriors.

2. b) Wilt Chamberlain
Philadelphia Warriors' Wilt Chamberlain hauled down 55 boards on November 24, 1960, against the Boston Celtics.

3. d) Vince Carter
Vince Carter of the Memphis Grizzlies turned 40 years old on January 26, 2017, during his 20th year in the league. The former dunk champion, nicknamed "Vinsanity" and "Air Canada," has played for six teams during his storied career.

Basketball Through Time!

1951
Nat "Sweetwater" Clifton is the first African-American contracted to play in the NBA.

1954
Minneapolis Lakers become first team to achieve three consecutive NBA titles, or a "three-peat."

1935
National Basketball League (NBL) is founded.

1949
The NBL and the BAA merge to form the NBA.

1891
Canadian James Naismith invents the game of basketball in a gymnasium in Massachusetts. He used peach baskets for hoops.

1951–52
The free-throw lane is widened from 6 feet to 12 feet.

1946
Basketball Association of America (BAA) is founded as a way for hockey arenas to fill open dates in their schedules.

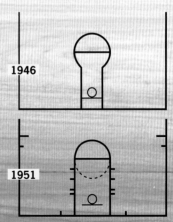

1946

1951

1970

Kareem Abdul-Jabbar, formerly Lew Alcindor, helps lead the Milwaukee Bucks to their only NBA championship. He is named finals MVP and league MVP, his first of six regular season MVPs.

1959

Bill Russell leads the Boston Celtics to an NBA final win, their first of eight consecutive wins. Russell will go on to win a total of 11 titles with the Celtics.

1976

The American Basketball Association (ABA), which was founded in 1967, merges with the NBA.

1962

Oscar Robertson becomes the first player to average a triple-double for the whole season.

1955

Danny Biasone invents the 24-second shot clock.

1971–72

The LA Lakers rattle off 33 straight wins over a three-month span, the most consecutive wins in a regular season.

1962

Wilt Chamberlain scores 100 points in one game, the modern day record that still stands.

1980

Magic Johnson and Larry Bird enter the NBA, sparking one of the league's greatest rivalries.

1986

The Boston Celtics go 40-1 at home during the regular season, the best home record in NBA history.

1983

The highest scoring game in NBA history occurs between the Detroit Pistons and the Denver Nuggets. The game finished 186–184, with Detroit winning in triple overtime.

1979

The three-point line is introduced to the NBA.

1984

Michael Jordan enters the league with the Chicago Bulls, setting the stage for six championships — two three-peats.

1982

The Denver Nuggets set an NBA record for most points per game, averaging an astonishing 126.5 points over the 1981–82 season.

1986

Michael Jordan goes off for 63 points in the playoffs, marking one of the great post-season performances in history.

1989

Dale Ellis plays 69 minutes — the most minutes in a single NBA game — in a quintuple-over-time thriller between the Seattle SuperSonics and the Milwaukee Bucks.

2000

"Vinsanity" is officially born when Toronto Raptors guard Vince Carter destroys the NBA Dunk Contest with a between-the-legs slam. The contest elevated him to superstar status and ushered in a new era for Canadian basketball.

1995

The Toronto Raptors and the Vancouver Grizzlies enter the NBA, marking the NBA's expansion into Canada.

1990

Scott Skiles sets the record for most assists in a single game, with 30.

1997

The first WNBA game is played on June 21 between the New York Liberty and the Los Angeles Sparks.

1996

The Women's National Basketball Association (WNBA) is officially formed.

2003

The San Antonio Spurs win their second title with the legendary duo of Tim Duncan and David Robinson. The Spurs go on to capture three more titles with Duncan.

2016

Kyrie Irving knocks down the game-winning shot in Game 7 of the NBA final, securing Cleveland's first basketball title and ending the city's championship drought — the longest in North American pro sports.

2012

LeBron James wins his first title. He appears in seven straight NBA finals from 2011 to 2017.

2010

Kobe Bryant leads the LA Lakers to another title win — his fifth and final ring. He was named NBA finals MVP twice in his career.

2005

Steve Nash of the Phoenix Suns is named MVP, the first Canadian to win the award. He follows it up with a second trophy the following season.

2016

The Golden State Warriors win their 73rd game, setting a new NBA record with a 73-9 regular season record.

2015

Klay Thompson drops 37 points in one quarter, hitting nine threes and setting a new NBA record.

2017

The NBA breaks the league record for most triple-doubles in a single season with 115. Russell Westbrook leads the league in scoring and averages a triple-double for the whole season, the first player to accomplish that feat since Oscar Robertson in 1962.

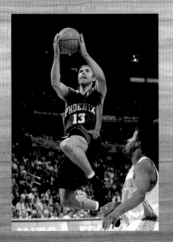

Player Profiles

20 Stephen Curry

28 Zach LaVine

30 Pau Gasol

32 DeMarcus Cousins

40 Russell Westbrook

42 Chris Paul

44 Zach Randolph

52 Carmelo Anthony

54 Dwight Howard

56 Klay Thompson

22 Anthony Davis

24 Dwyane Wade

26 LeBron James

34 Kristaps Porzingis

36 Kevin Durant

38 Jeremy Lin

46 DeMar DeRozan

48 Andrew Wiggins

50 Kyle Korver

58 Isaiah Thomas

60 Dirk Nowitzki

62 Kyrie Irving

Steph Curry makes it rain.

Stephen Curry
Golden State Warriors Point Guard

He owns the biggest smile in the NBA. It's a goofy grin, one that usually emerges after he hits another of his seemingly limitless rainmakers from three-point land. Stephen Curry's got the "It factor": a set of skills and other attributes so hard to describe that players simply have "It" or they don't, and when a player does have "It" everyone knows.

Steph is the son of retired NBA player Dell Curry. Dell played for many teams during his pro career, but none influenced the young Curry more than the Toronto Raptors. Steph was just entering high school, and Curry Senior was playing with the likes of Vince Carter and Tracy McGrady. Steph followed them around at practices and shoot-arounds, and some of their skills definitely rubbed off on the young Curry.

Curry is slight in stature — 6-foot-3 and 190 pounds — and was passed over by major college programs. He always had a sweet shot, however, and he continued to hone it at Davidson College, where he led the tiny school to the Elite Eight. When he hit the NBA with the Golden State Warriors, where three-pointers had become the staple of the team's offense, it was a match made in heaven.

Curry has been can't-miss-TV since winning the 2014–15 championship with the Warrlors, and his face is everywhere. He's now the NBA's most popular player and a two-time league MVP. In 2014–15 he set the record for the most postseason three-pointers with 98. The record was previously held by the great Reggie Miller.

30

It looks like a video game is being played when the mouth-guard-chewing point guard is on the court. It's like he's *always* on fire, and Curry's shooting accuracy is destroying records. If he's not hitting a trey off the dribble or knocking down half-court shots at the buzzer, he's bouncing the ball between his legs or soaring to the hoop for a layup as gracefully as a ballet dancer.

The Warriors started the 2015–16 season 24-0 before losing their first game and finished with a staggering 73-9 record. This record bested Michael Jordan's dominant 1995–96 season with the Chicago Bulls. Those Bulls claimed the championship, and many expected the Warriors would do the same, but LeBron James and the Cleveland Cavaliers won three straight games to take the title.

Along with Klay Thompson and new recruit Kevin Durant, the Warriors boast three of the four best shooters in the NBA. In 2017 the sharpshooting team took back the title from the Cavs, and Curry proved he's still got "It."

HOOPS FOR HUMANITY!

Over the last four years, for every three-pointer Curry has made, he's donated three life-saving bed nets to the charity Nothing But Nets, which helps protect poor families in Africa from malaria.

Anthony Davis
New Orleans Pelicans
Power Forward

23

Born in 1993, Anthony Davis is one of the youngest superstars in the league. And while 2016–17 was his fifth NBA season with the New Orleans Pelicans, it feels like he's been around a lot longer than that.

You probably recognize him instantly by his signature uni-brow, but behind the brow is a bunch of bright stats. The 6-foot-11, 253-pound power forward has led the NBA in blocks twice, and he's been named an All-Star four times. In the first game of the 2014–15 season, Davis pummeled the Orlando Magic with thunderous stats: 26 points, 17 rebounds, 9 blocks, 3 steals and 2 assists. Those kinds of across-the-board numbers are stupendous! He finished the year averaging 24.4 points and 10.2 rebounds per game.

But Davis wasn't always this big and good. In fact, he was so small as a high school freshman in Chicago — 5-foot-9 and 130 pounds — that he started as a guard. When he experienced a huge growth spurt in his teens, he became a player with a big body but with the skills of a smaller player. That combo, combined with some hard work, vaulted him to the top of the class. After leading Kentucky to the 2012 NCAA Championship as a freshman, Davis was selected first overall in the draft by the Pelicans.

Davis is part of the new wave of NBA stars — talented players who can play multiple positions and be trusted to deliver in pressure-packed situations. The Pelicans are banking their future on Davis after signing him to a five-year, $145 million contract, and Davis is making a difference on and off the court in New Orleans. He's hosted bowling fundraisers for the local YMCA and has twice won the Seasonlong Kia Community Assist Award through his charity, AD's Flight Academy. Davis calls winning that award "a great honor and a blessing," and he donated the award money to helping restore Louisiana's coastal wetlands.

On the court, this gentle giant goes into "beast mode," dunking over opponents and swatting away shots at will with his long arms. Davis blocked nearly three shots per game in 2014–15 while posting an 80.5% free-throw percentage. During four games that postseason, he chipped in 31.5 points and 11 rebounds per contest. Injuries hampered the superstar in 2015–16, but he still set career highs in rebounds and three-point shooting, which means he is crafting a well-rounded game beyond points and blocks.

SCARY HAIRY | Did you know that Davis, who graced the cover of *Sports Illustrated* during his third NBA season, trademarked the phrase "Fear the Brow"? That means no one else can use it without his permission.

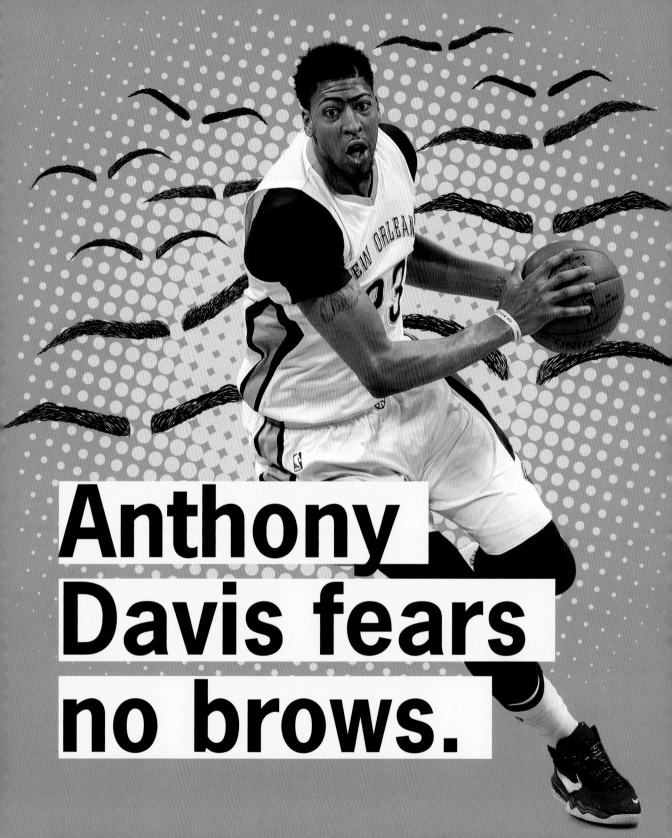

Anthony Davis fears no brows.

Dwyane Wade is Homecoming King.

Dwyane Wade
Chicago Bulls
Shooting Guard

Dwyane Wade has come home to Chicago. He grew up and played his youth ball in the city before landing at nearby Marquette for college. And then he left, drafted by the Miami Heat fifth overall in 2003. Now a former league MVP and bona fide superstar, Wade is finishing his career where it all started.

In Chicago, Wade had to overcome more than most people to become not only a star in the NBA but a role model as well. His mother was sent to jail when he was a teenager, and he fought hard to ensure he didn't follow in her footsteps. He flourished at Marquette and announced himself to NBA teams at the upcoming draft by dropping a triple-double in the NCAA Final Four against Kentucky. By the time he started for Miami, he was a household name, and the praise piled up.

"D-Wade" won his first title alongside Shaquille O'Neal in 2006, winning MVP that same season on 27.2 points, 6.7 dimes and 5.7 boards per game; he was simply the best guard in the game at the time. He established Miami as a constant contender, and when the Heat brought in his good buddies LeBron James and Chris Bosh, he earned two more rings as part of a skilled offensive trio.

But it wasn't all smooth sailing for Wade. He's had to play through many injuries to his hips and knees. However, when people thought the injuries might take him out in 2008–09, he posted 30.2 points per game, capturing the scoring title. He's now sailing into the top 40 of all-time in points — impressive for a guard who wasn't considered a top player coming out of high school. In his last season in Miami (2015–16), he took the Heat all the way to Game 7 of the second round, shooting over 50% from the three-point line. It was a huge effort in a losing cause.

Beyond the game, it's the little things D-Wade does that make him a star worth imitating. "My life is bigger than basketball," he says on his website, and the 12-time All-Star's charity work, assisting thousands of kids in at-risk situations, speaks to his spirit of giving back to the community. Miami will miss Wade on the court, but even more in the community, where he would regularly make public appearances, especially on holidays, to assist those less fortunate. Quite simply, Wade is one of those stars who makes everyone around him better — on the court and in life.

Wade's three rings, scoring title and MVP all position him to go down as a player who transcended the game, but his work off the court has proven good guys can finish first.

SOLE OF HIS GAME

Wade has one of the most unusual shoe deals in the league. He's signed with Chinese company Li-Ning, who have created a brand just for him called, Way of Wade.

LeBron James
Cleveland Cavaliers
Small Forward

23

LeBron James is the most exciting player in the NBA and has been a must-watch athlete since he joined the league straight out of high school in 2003.

Drafted first overall by the Cleveland Cavaliers, James came into the league as a teenager with the body of a man. At 6-foot-8 and 250 pounds, he's bigger than many football players, but his amazing speed and skill with the ball means James can play guard or forward.

The Ohio native's time in Cleveland put NBA basketball back on the map in that city, where success (in any sport) has been hard to come by. But he didn't win his first championships in Cleveland. He won them in Miami with the Heat. He and Chris Bosh teamed with Miami superstar Dwyane Wade for four seasons and won two NBA titles.

Miami Heat fans had their hopes set on a dynasty, but when James became a free agent he returned to Cleveland. In a letter he wrote for *Sports Illustrated,* he promised to turn the Cavs into champions.

LeBron nearly kept his promise in his first season back, carrying the injury-laden Cavs to the 2015 final. Cleveland may have lost to the Golden State Warriors that year, but LeBron's performance was legendary; he led *both* teams in points, assists and rebounds.

He took his revenge on the Warriors the next season. With Cleveland one win away from being eliminated from the final, James and company scrapped back from a 3-1 series deficit to win the 2016 championship. In those three winning games, James hit 41 points on back-to-back nights, scored a triple-double in Game 7 and will always be remembered for "The Block." With the game tied and Andre Iguodala set to score for Golden State, LeBron ran the length of the floor and swatted the ball from his hands. Seconds later, James' teammate Kyrie Irving hit the game-winning shot.

LeBron's career average of 27 points make him the only player alive who could catch Kareem Abdul-Jabbar's all-time points record of 38,387. His averages are also nearly as good or better in some categories than the player many call the best of all time — Michael Jordan. But James will need more than three championship rings to convince people he is the best ever.

Except in Cleveland. James doesn't have to convince anyone at home of how great he is. LeBron is a staple in the Cleveland area as a mentor and leader through the LeBron James Family Foundation, and his phrase, "Just Another Kid from Akron," can be seen everywhere in the city. The message is that kids can be anything they want — even the greatest player in the NBA — if they set their goals and follow through.

OVER-ACHIEVER | LeBron has already been named MVP four times in his career, won two Olympic gold medals with Team USA and even hosted *Saturday Night Live*!

LeBron James is King Basketball.

Zach LaVine
Minnesota Timberwolves
Shooting Guard

8

Two slam dunk contests, two wins — that's what Zach LaVine has already accomplished in his short NBA career. What's next? One thing's for certain: the Minnesota Timberwolves shooting guard will be soaring for years to come.

LaVine grew up in Washington State and starred as the point guard for Bothell High School, where he averaged a cool 28.5 points per game and was named Washington's Mr. Basketball in 2013. The future dunk machine's path to the NBA went through the halls of UCLA, where superstars Kevin Love and Russell Westbrook also played their college ball.

Zach played just one season for UCLA before being drafted 13th overall in 2014 by the Timberwolves. LaVine's a perfect fit for the new fast, high-scoring style of NBA play. At 6-foot-5 and 185 pounds, he's lean and efficient, able to drop threes and dunk over opponents at will. He played in all 82 regular season games in 2015–16 and averaged 14 points and 28 minutes per game.

LaVine made his mark on the league and gained fans of all ages with his second-straight dunk contest win against Orlando Magic forward Aaron Gordon. Doing things no one has ever seen — like wrapping the ball behind his back and throwing it down reverse style — LaVine proved he's on another level. That February night in Toronto, LaVine provided a spectacular show. The contest was a back and forth affair, but the high-flying guard emerged victorious, leaping from (almost) the free-throw line and putting the ball through his legs to finish off Gordon. Now he's an Internet legend thanks to his nods to the 1996 film *Space Jam* and Michael Jordan's legendary dunks.

LaVine's also a big personality in the local community, and he soars above and beyond when it comes to helping others. In his second year, the shooting guard received an NBA Community Assist Award for his charitable work with the Metro Deaf School in Saint Paul, Minnesota, where he spent many quality hours with students and to which he donated $10,000.

LaVine is getting better with each season. His three-point shooting improved to 39% in 2015–16, and he ended the campaign on a tear, knocking down back-to-back 28-point games late in the season. In December 2016, he notched a career-high 40 points in a game against the Sacramento Kings. There are things the talented guard can improve upon — such as playing smarter and through contact — but these things will come with experience. In fact, as Minnesota's top picks mature, playoff contention will become a reality for the young Timberwolves.

PRO ATHLETE PEDIGREE

Like teammate Andrew Wiggins, LaVine's dad is a former pro athlete. Paul LaVine was a football player in the NFL for one season with the Seattle Seahawks.

Zach LaVine
believes
he can fly.

Pau Gasol's brains match his brawn.

Pau Gasol
San Antonio Spurs
Center

Spain's Pau Gasol, like many European big men, was a strong NBA prospect. He arrived with a well-rounded game, thanks to his time playing in the European pro loop as a young man. Now approaching the end of his career, he's crafted an eye-popping résumé for an international player. He's also proved to be one of the most interesting players off the court.

The 7-foot center now plays for the San Antonio Spurs, but Gasol began in Barcelona, where his mother worked as a doctor. It inspired a lifelong interest in medicine, and Gasol almost followed in her footsteps. But his talent on the hard court couldn't be ignored, and he quickly jumped from the Spanish league to the NBA. After being drafted third overall in 2001, he was named Rookie of the Year while playing with the Memphis Grizzlies. (His younger brother Marc followed Pau to the NBA, and he is now the starting center for the Grizz.)

Pau's career flourished in Memphis, but early playoff exits dampened his achievements. After being traded to the Los Angeles Lakers, he won two NBA championships alongside one of the greatest players of his generation, Kobe Bryant. Gasol's post presence in LA's triangle offense helped drive the team's success.

Kobe recently said of his former teammate, "Pau sees the game many, many layers ahead," citing the center's intelligence above his physical gifts. Plus, his combination of size and quickness means Gasol can post up against bigger

men, step back and hit a jumper or send a terrific pass over a double team for a bucket. With these moves he's added two Olympic medals to his trophy case, playing for his native Spain alongside his brother.

Gasol's knowledge covers many different fields. He speaks several languages and includes opera, playing piano and reading among his cultural pursuits. He regularly visits children's hospitals, not only because he loves interacting with kids but also because he enjoys learning about different surgeries and techniques.

And he hasn't let his long list of interests distract him on the court, where he set a career high in rebounds with 11.8 per game in 2014–15 while playing with the Chicago Bulls. There he had back-to-back seasons of double-double averages and two All-Star Game appearances.

Gasol is blessed with strength, skill and smarts. This winning combination has allowed him to become a successful star for two decades. He's hoping a swan song with the Spurs will cement his legacy.

TASTE FOR SUCCESS

Gasol is good friends with another Spanish sports star, tennis player Rafael Nadal. Along with pop star Enrique Iglesias, they opened a restaurant in Madrid called Tatel.

DeMarcus Cousins has serious moves.

DeMarcus Cousins
New Orleans Pelicans
Center

DeMarcus Cousins is gigantic. At 6-foot-11 and 270 pounds, he isn't the kind of guy you'd expect to have a soft touch with the ball and agility on the court. But that is exactly what Cousins possesses. His college coach at the University of Kentucky was so surprised by the big man's moves that he was nicknamed "Boogie" for his ability to shimmy on the court. But with a body as big as his, Cousins can also dominate below the hoop and in the physical areas on the court. His blend of seemingly opposite talents is why he's managed to dance his way to NBA stardom.

Growing up in Mobile, Alabama, Cousins was already a humongous 6-foot-4 by grade 7, and despite his affection for football, basketball became his true calling. In only his second year playing on the hard court, Cousins was the number-one high school player in the state for his age! The center was recruited heavily by college powerhouses, and he eventually settled on Kentucky because of their reputation for taking high school stars and turning them into NBA-ready players in just one year.

At Kentucky, he put up averages of 15 points and 10 boards per game en route to KU making the Elite Eight in the NCAA tournament. But Cousins' sights were always set on the NBA. He was just too big, too good and too promising, and he entered the NBA draft after his first year at KU. He was drafted fifth overall in 2010 by the Sacramento Kings. In California he thrived as the offensive focal point for six and a half seasons until a blockbuster move on All-Star

weekend 2017 sent him packing to the New Orleans Pelicans. Now just two hours from his hometown, Boogie's playing alongside Anthony Davis, another big, young player, and together they form a formidable partnership.

Cousins gets a bad rap as a hothead on the court, but those close to him say people misunderstand his fiery, competitive drive to win. Cousins volunteers much of his time in the community and runs Camp Boogie every summer for kids to play ball. He also sponsored a discussion between police and the community in his hometown of Mobile with the slogan "Break the Silence, Build the Trust."

In 2014–15 Cousins established then-career highs in all offensive categories, with 24.1 points, 12.7 rebounds, 3.6 assists, 1.5 steals and 1.8 blocks. The following season, the center added a three-point shot to his already incredible arsenal. He finished the 2015–16 season averaging 26.9 points per game, bettering his personal best and finishing fourth overall in the league. In 2016–17 he was one of the NBA's top scorers again. Cousins also won a gold medal as a member of the 2016 Olympic U.S. men's basketball team.

FLASHY FEET

Boogie's known for wearing a variety of shoes — LeBrons, Jordans, you name it — and he isn't afraid of flashy colors. And in case you were wondering, he wears a size 17.

Kristaps Porzingis
New York Knicks Center

I t's 2015 in Brooklyn, New York, and Kristaps Porzingis, the 7-foot-3, 240-pound Latvian phenom, has just had his name called by the New York Knicks as the fourth-overall pick in the NBA draft. Almost immediately Knicks fans turn into boo birds — even the kids in the crowd taunt the team for selecting this virtually unknown center. Over the course of Porzingis' rookie season, however, he will provide a master class in silencing the critics.

Porzingis finished his freshman year in New York with 14.3 points per game, 7.3 rebounds and 1.9 blocks. He appeared in 72 games and finished second in Rookie of the Year voting to the talented Karl-Anthony Towns.

Porzingis had such an impressive NBA debut partly because he took extra time to hone his skills in the professional Spanish league, playing for three seasons against older veterans even though he could have entered the NBA draft. It's paid off.

Few centers can match up against his size and speed. Porzingis' dribbling skills are akin to point guards Isaiah Thomas and D'Angelo Russell, and he is a top jumper, nearly able to touch the top of the backboard. He also has a budding three-point shot. In his rookie year he hit 81 of 243 shots taken from behind the arc. That 33% success rate is impressive for a 7-footer.

Another contributing factor to the center's success in New York is that his family all moved to the Big Apple for his rookie season. Being able to learn the language and customs of a new country together with his family was a comfort for Porzingis. It also helped to have his dad act as his manager and one of his brothers as his agent (and both are tall, too!).

In the off-season after his rookie campaign, Porzingis returned to his hometown of Liepaja in Latvia to run his first basketball camp. It was a big deal for a country of just two million that has never had an NBA star of Porzingis' stature. At another camp just outside of New York, he said about the kids, "Some of them don't even come up to my knees. I'm huge."

Yes, he certainly is. And Knicks fans know it, many of them wearing jerseys touting his stature as "PORZINGOD." The NBA should be on alert: on both the offensive and defensive ends, Porzingis is a rare talent.

NOT SO SAD ANYMORE | Did you know Porzingis played a friendly 1-on-1 with the kid dubbed "Crying Knicks Fan," who famously booed Porzingis at the draft? The center is now his favorite player.

Kristaps Porzingis puts the "big" in Big Apple.

Kevin Durant
Golden State Warriors
Small Forward

35

With his super skinny legs and arms, young Kevin Durant didn't fit the mold of a future superstar. But what the gangly forward lacked in strength and size, he made up for in sheer talent and dedication.

Today Durant is one of a handful of players competing for the unofficial title of "best basketball player on the planet." He's still got a long, lanky body, but he's figured out how to use his length to his advantage. He's also one of the purest shooters in the NBA. At 6-foot-9 and 240 pounds and with ball skills that rival anyone in the NBA, Durant has led the league in scoring four times. He is also one of only seven players to reach the 50-40-90 club (a shooting percentage at or above 50% for field goals, 40% for three-pointers and 90% for free throws during an entire NBA regular season), which he did in 2012–13.

Quiet and humble on and off the court, Durant led the Oklahoma City Thunder from the team's beginning until the end of the 2015–16 season. He became the franchise player for the relocated Seattle SuperSonics immediately after being drafted second overall in 2007. Fans love his nice-guy approach and coaches love his shooting stroke, his hard-to-protect fadeaway, his lethal 20-footer and his ability to play shooting guard or small forward.

Oklahoma was a bottom-five team in Durant's rookie season, and alongside point guard Russell Westbrook, he transformed the club into a feared contender. But after an embarrassing home court loss in Game 6 of the 2016 Western Conference final — and subsequent series loss — Durant is now with the Golden State Warriors and has proven to be the piece they needed to reclaim the NBA championship, deservedly winning the title of Finals MVP in 2017. Rival defenses must shake in their boots when preparing to face the Warriors because their starting five includes Durant, Steph Curry and Klay Thompson.

Durant was raised by his mother and grandmother in a rough neighborhood and has maintained a close bond with his family. When he won the NBA MVP award in 2013–14 (a season in which he put up 32 points per game, 7.4 rebounds and 5.5 assists), he thanked his mom, tearing up when he said, "You the real MVP."

One of Durant's passions now that he is a top basketball player is to give kids in tough circumstances the opportunity to play sports and excel in school. One of his biggest projects is Build It and They Will Ball, which develops high-end basketball courts for underprivileged kids across the United States.

#FOR THEWIN

Durant's gone global. He starred in the documentary *The Offseason*, which followed him for an entire summer, and he also has a whopping 15.5 million Twitter followers (@KDTrey5).

Kevin Durant breaks the mold.

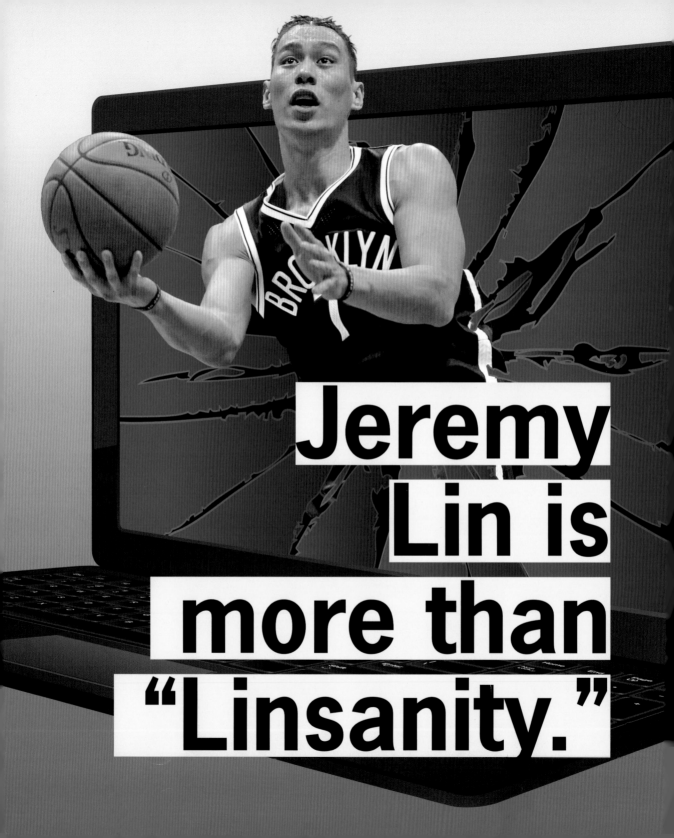

Jeremy Lin is more than "Linsanity."

Jeremy Lin
Brooklyn Nets
Point Guard

"Linsanity" took the NBA by storm in 2012 and quickly became a worldwide phenomenon. The NBA had never seen anything quite like the almost instantaneous worldwide fever Jeremy Lin inspired. One day, he was an unknown backup point guard with the New York Knicks. The next, he was the biggest thing in the game. He's now a talented point guard for the Brooklyn Nets, but his magical run in February 2012 will almost certainly be his basketball legacy.

Lin may not have been pegged for stardom, but he was always unique. Gifted athletically and intellectually, he played his college ball at an Ivy League school, Harvard, where he averaged 12.3 points per game. He wasn't drafted to the NBA, but he persevered, turning heads while playing in the Summer League. The Golden State Warriors signed him to his first NBA contract in 2010.

Lin didn't last long with his hometown Warriors though, and by the middle of the 2011–12 season, he was with the New York Knicks, where chance thrust him into the spotlight.

In early February, with superstars Carmelo Anthony and Amar'e Stoudemire both out of the lineup, Lin seized a starring role. He posted jaw-dropping numbers over the next weeks, including a 38-point, 7-assist effort versus the LA Lakers. The Knicks, who started the lockout-shortened season with only eight wins in their first 23 games, took off, winning seven games in a row and 10 of 13 to finish February with an

18-18 record and a shot at the playoffs. The whole league took notice, and Linsanity was born.

Lin graced the cover of *Sports Illustrated* twice (back to back issues!) and had the second best jersey sales in the NBA — all while only playing 26 games as a starter before being injured. Linsanity raced across the globe, and the impact was particularly large in China. His face appeared on the front pages of countless newspapers and the cover of the Asian edition of *Time* magazine.

While things aren't as crazy anymore, the undrafted guard has had a better career than predicted. From New York he went to the Houston Rockets and then to the Charlotte Hornets, where his hard work was always appreciated by his teammates. His new three-year, $36 million deal with the Brooklyn Nets brings him back to the Big Apple and an opportunity to play top minutes. Linsanity may have passed, but Lin continues to have a massive impact on the Asian-American community, which has few heroes in the NBA.

EAST MEETS WEST

Lin heads the Jeremy Lin Foundation, and he visited China (where his grandparents were born) in 2015 with NBA Cares to meet schoolchildren in the city of Shenzhen.

Russell Westbrook
Oklahoma City Thunder
Point Guard

Russell Westbrook has traveled a long way to get where he is today — NBA superstardom. Growing up, he was smaller than the other kids on the court, and he wasn't in demand by college recruiters. He defied the odds, however, and managed to make it to UCLA. There he thrived, becoming the 6-foot-3, bold leader on the hard court we know today. He is also the heart and soul of the Oklahoma City Thunder.

The point guard grew up in a close-knit family in tough inner-city Los Angeles, and his parents scratched and clawed to stay afloat, ensuring Westbrook stayed off the streets. His hardworking parents were determined for their two boys to succeed. It worked, and the point guard still talks to them before every NBA game.

Being smaller than most other players on his high school team, Westbrook made up for his size by developing a strong work ethic. His father put him through intense workouts when he was young: 500 shots in the gym, sit-ups, pull-ups — it was old-school preparation. Then he grew five inches, and the star power inside him was unleashed. Westbrook's style of play came to be known for its unforgiving pace; coaches called him a "crazed dog" on the court. Westbrook once said his father taught him that "when the game starts, the basketball is your only friend."

All of this has translated into the player you see on the NBA floor today: Westbrook's no-holds-barred approach makes him quicker than anyone else. He wears number zero, uncommon for an NBA player, revealing his unique personality.

His passion and competitiveness for the game are legendary. He rarely takes a play off, let alone a night. When former teammate Kevin Durant was injured in 2014–15, Westbrook stepped up. He recorded four triple-doubles in a row, the first player since Michael Jordan to do so, and scored 54 points in one of the final games of the season. In 2016–17 he set or matched career highs in all the major categories averaging 31.9 points, 10.7 rebounds and 10.4 assists. Oklahoma is now Westbrook's team thanks to Durant's departure to the Golden State Warriors. The world will be watching to see if he can be the man.

"The man" is a title he already holds in many Oklahoma communities, where he runs literacy programs. In 2014–15 he received the NBA Community Assist Award. He even donated the car he won as MVP of the 2015 All-Star Game to a single mother putting herself through college.

The Oklahoma point guard clearly has a pretty big heart, on the court and off. With his perseverance, leadership and dedication, it is finally Westbrook's time to lead the Thunder as their premier player.

STYLE SAVVY | In 2015 *Sports Illustrated* called Westbrook "the most stylish man in the NBA." He's even got his own fashion line, simply called Westbrook.

Russell Westbrook is the man for the job.

Chris Paul
Los Angeles Clippers
Point Guard

Chris Paul just might be the friendliest player in the NBA. Need proof? Watch how many opponents shake his hand before each game. That's because Paul's a gracious competitor and has been influential in shaping the next generation of point guards.

Paul's Elite Guard basketball camp gives 30 of the nation's top young point guards the opportunity to learn the tools of the trade from him — a player many consider to be the best point guard in the game. Current NBA players like Kemba Walker of the Charlotte Hornets and Trey Burke of the Washington Wizards are now succeeding thanks in part to Paul's mentorship.

Paul's play routinely drives opponents mad. He's led the NBA in steals six times and has finished in the top three another four times in his career. His playmaking is legendary, and he's led the NBA pack four times in assists. He's now playing with the Los Angeles Clippers alongside superstar power forward Blake Griffin, and this talented twosome matches up well against any duo on any NBA team. The Clippers are probably the best team Paul has ever played on,

which, many fans hope, will help the star finally win a championship.

He's been unlucky in the playoffs for most of his career, but he's proved he has the mettle to play in big moments. In 2015 he hit a game-winning shot in the final seconds of Game 7 of Round 1 versus the reigning San Antonio Spurs. But a first-round exit in 2016 means Paul is still hungry to prove he's got NBA championships in his blood.

Paul is as much a leader in the community as he is on the court. He's won the NBA's Community Assist Award four times, and his CP3 Foundation provides scholarships to Wake Forest University, where he played his college ball. The point guard also assists Habitat for Humanity, Feed the Children, the Special Olympics and so many other causes that it's hard to keep track!

All of it — his charity work, slick passing, crazy crossovers and alley-oops — make Paul one of the most likeable players in the NBA. He may run the court like a drill sergeant, barking orders and waving his finger at his teammates, but even when the game is intense, he's always respectful. And his basketball IQ is through the roof.

Whether on the court or during his annual bowling tournament in the off-season, Paul is a leader in all aspects of the game and a truly special player.

FRESH KICKS

Want to own pair of Paul's kicks? There's plenty to choose from in his signature Jordan collection. Each one has a signature Chevron symbol that honors his grandfather. Paul himself has an entire walk-in closet in his house just for his Jordans!

Chris Paul guides on and off the court.

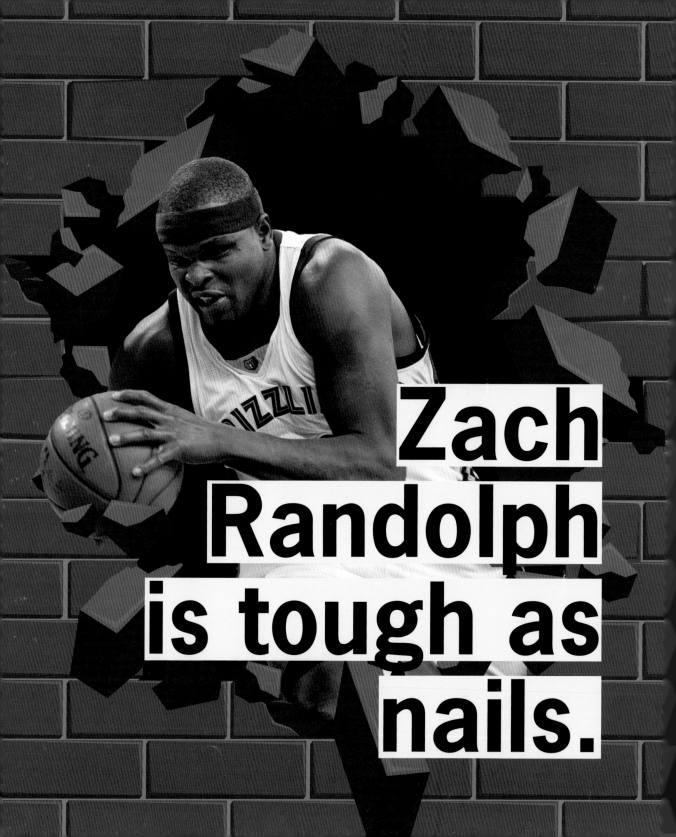

Zach Randolph is tough as nails.

Zach Randolph
Memphis Grizzlies
Power Forward

Zach Randolph built his career on hard work. You'll find "Z-Bo" below the basket, outworking the other guy and rebounding balls against bigger competition. That's been his trademark since high school, when he led his team to Indiana's state championships twice. Now at 6-foot-9 and 260 pounds, Randolph is built like a big rig. He is a key figure in the resurgence of the Memphis Grizzlies — now a top contender in the NBA — and his selfless play has helped teammates, like center Marc Gasol and point guard Mike Conley, thrive.

Z-Bo is one of the hardest working players in the game — he's a dependable double-double guy each and every night. He's also one of the nicest athletes off the court, despite the aggressive on-court attitude that's led to more than one technical foul. Randolph understands struggle, having grown up poor with only his mother, Mae, to support him and his siblings. He was one of a handful of freshmen to start on the varsity team at his Indiana high school. He rose through the basketball ranks in spite of his difficult home life and the constant demand to prove himself to older ball players.

Success continued once the power forward jumped to the NCAA. In his freshman year at Michigan State, Randolph and his team made it all the way to the Final Four. In 2001 he was a first-round selection who was drafted 19th overall by the Portland Trail Blazers. Randolph was named the NBA's most improved player in 2004 and quickly established himself as one of the league's toughest players in the key.

Over his NBA career, Randolph has averaged nearly 17 points and 10 rebounds per game, and he's made the All-Star Team twice. The 2016–17 season was his eighth for the Grizz after short stints with the New York Knicks and the LA Clippers. Z-Bo continues to work hard as usual, averaging nearly 30 minutes per game and wearing his trademark headband and number 50.

Randolph also gives back whenever he can. In 2013 he received the NBA Community Assist Award twice. In addition to helping out back in his hometown of Indiana, he is active in the Memphis community, helping residents pay their electricity bills and rescuing local dogs. The 35-year-old goes about his business just like he does on the court, with a big smile, a humble work ethic and a tough-as-nails attitude.

In 2015 one team executive said about Randolph's career in Memphis, "He's not just liked here, he's beloved."

FAN FAVE | In 2015, when Memphis faced the Portland Trail Blazers in the first round of the playoffs, Randolph purchased 300 tickets for fans to attend the game for free. Now that's impressive!

DeMar DeRozan
Toronto Raptors
Shooting Guard

10

Demar DeRozan is a new breed of superstar: humble and quiet, he's a player who goes about his business with simplicity. That doesn't mean he can't take over a game; it means he waits for his moments to post up, drive to the basket or knock down a fadeaway. The rest of the time DeRozan plays a team game, and the Toronto Raptors are better for his ability to let others shine.

DeRozan grew up in Compton, California, where basketball quickly became his calling. He was dunking the ball in sixth grade and was the best player in the region by the time he was a teenager. In his freshman year of high school, DeRozan was already averaging 26 points per contest, and now his old school gym is named in his honor.

DeRozan played one year of NCAA ball with University of Southern California before entering the NBA draft, where he was chosen ninth overall in 2009 by the Raptors. He jumped from college early to the pros to better take care of his mother, who suffers from lupus.

DeRozan is cresting into his prime years, and his new big-money contract ($139 million over five years, one of the highest contracts in the NBA) won't change the personality of the soft-spoken shooting guard, who has spent his entire career with Toronto. He quietly goes about his business night after night, and in 2016–17 he had his best season to date, averaging a career-high 27.3 points and five rebounds per game and shooting 84% from the stripe.

In early December 2015 he was named Eastern Conference Player of the Week for the first time in his career, after dropping 24.0 points per game and shooting 91.9% from the free-throw line. His defense also greatly improved in the 2015–16 season. That growth in DeRozan's overall game helped lead the Raps to 11 straight victories mid-season, which tied a franchise record, and he's finally seeing some playoff success with teammate Kyle Lowry. The two carried the Raps to the Eastern Conference final for the first time in franchise history.

"Loyalty, that's what I'm based off of," he said in 2014, as the Raptors began turning into a postseason contender. He backed it up with his long-term deal to stay in the city that gave him his start.

DeRozan has won over the Toronto community by being actively involved with First Book Canada, a literacy program for youth — he credits his parents' insistence on education as one of the keys to his success as a player. Coach Dwane Casey calls DeRozan "a student of the game" and a "basketball nerd." That's maybe the highest compliment any player can get from a coach.

ON THE BLACKTOP

DeRozan is one of the mainstays in the Drew League, a laid-back summer competition held in his hometown of Los Angeles. Young players line up in droves to see NBA stars like D-Ro compete against each other outside of their NBA teams.

DeMar DeRozan is Captain Canada.

Andrew Wiggins
Minnesota Timberwolves
Small Forward

22

Andrew Wiggins often wears a big smile. He loves playing basketball, and the 2014–15 Rookie of the Year and number-one overall draft pick has positioned himself to become one of the NBA's great superstars. In other words, there are plenty of reasons for Wiggins' wide smile.

His career began north of the border, outside Toronto, where the young Wiggins fast became the top high schooler in Canada. He was so good that he was recruited by the leading U.S. prep school to further hone his skills. There he worked on combining his agility and ridiculous 44-inch vertical leap with his natural size and skill.

The quiet Canadian may not be the flashiest NBA star quite yet, but he's finding his form and leading the Minnesota Timberwolves into a new era. The 6-foot-8, 199-pound small forward started all 82 games in his first NBA season, averaging 16.9 points, 4.6 rebounds and 2.1 assists per game. In 2015–16 his point production ticked up. He dropped 32 against the 76ers early in the season, and then he scored 35 against the Cleveland Cavaliers — the team that drafted him before shuffling him off to Minnesota. He's created chemistry with fellow teammates Ricky Rubio and Zach LaVine, and things are looking bright in Minnesota.

Wiggins' arsenal includes a classic jump stop that he uses to freeze defenders as he takes off for the rim. The small forward still has a mountain to climb before being crowned an NBA superstar, but he's well on his way to achieving elite status with a 2016–17 season average of 23.6 points and games like his 2015–16 late-season gem against the Golden State Warriors — where he scored 32 in Minnesota's overtime win. He's risen from 91st to 67th on *Sports Illustrated*'s Top 100 list. With the emergence of fellow Timberwolves teammate Karl-Anthony Towns as 2016 Rookie of the Year, Wiggins is primed to excel on a talented team focused on growth.

Wiggins grew up in a tight-knit, sports-focused family — both of his parents were athletes — which has helped him learn some of what it takes to succeed. He has already made himself a positive role model for young fans who would be well served imitating his smooth style. And even if he does slip a little, Wiggins' work ethic will save him. He's logged more game minutes at his age than anyone in NBA history except for LeBron James. That's impressive company, and good news for one of the NBA's up and coming stars.

OH, CANADA!

Wiggins is from Brampton, Ontario, a suburb of Toronto, and he's not the only Canadian from the area in the NBA. Canada is producing NBA-ready talent at a remarkable pace, and players such as Nick Stauskas, Jamal Murray and Cory Joseph are just a few of the rising stars.

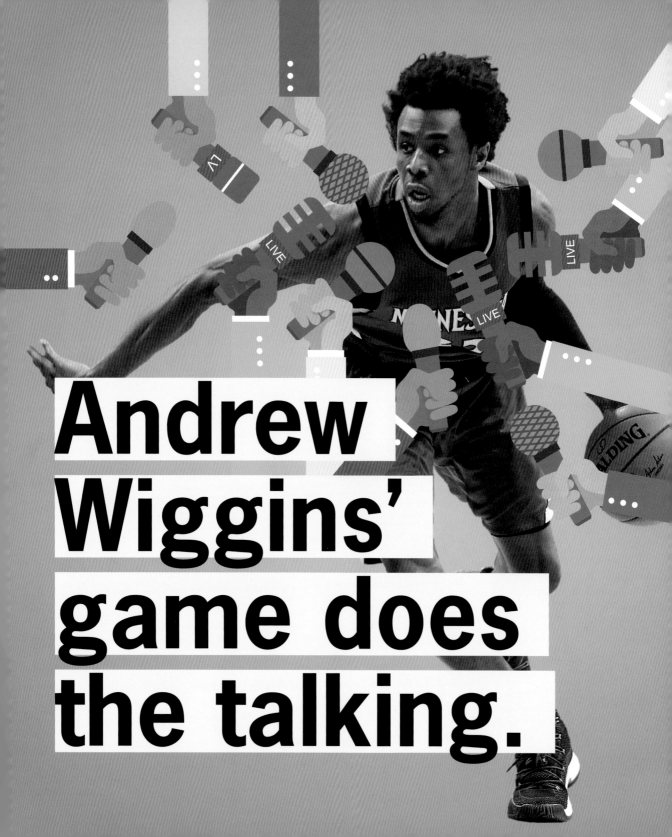

Andrew Wiggins' game does the talking.

Kyle Korver is a three-point machine.

Kyle Korver
Cleveland Cavaliers
Shooting Guard

Kyle Korver is one of the best shooters in the NBA, and he's on track to be one of the greatest ever. In 2009–10 he set the record for highest three-point shooting percentage in the history of the game (53.6%). And to think he was drafted 51st overall in 2003!

In 2014–15, at 34 years old, Korver nailed nearly 50% of his shots from behind the arc while in a starting role for the Atlanta Hawks after years coming off the bench. Korver credits his late career success to a strange sport — paddle boarding. LeBron James is a fan of the lights-out shooter, too, and during the 2016–17 season the Cleveland Cavaliers picked up Korver to fill the void left by J. R. Smith, who got hurt earlier in the season. Kyle's yet another weapon in the dominant Cavs' arsenal.

Korver comes from a basketball family: his parents and siblings have all played at high levels and are all great shooters. It's in the Korvers' genes, but success like Kyle's doesn't come without a phenomenal work ethic.

Korver is obsessed with shooting naturally, meaning he wants the stroke of his shot to be one fluid motion without the hitches and jerks of some NBA shooters. To help him shoot consistently every time, Korver created his own 20-point shooting checklist that includes notes on his stance and arm angle — things he constantly reminds himself to check every time he shoots the ball. Korver also ends every single practice by hitting 10 straight free throws and three treys from the top of the arc. For most of us, that would take all night. But when you're as good as Korver, hitting that many in a row

becomes routine — which is why he sticks to his practice methods.

Both Kyle's father and grandfather were pastors, and Korver has taken a keen interest in charities in every city he's played in, including Philadelphia, Salt Lake City, Chicago, Atlanta and, currently, Cleveland.

Between 2012 and 2014 Korver set the then NBA record for most consecutive games with a three-pointer (127). He shot 93% from the stripe in 2013–14, and he was a constant threat from behind the arc, which helped the Hawks reach the Eastern Conference final the following season — the first time since 1970. When the Cavaliers picked up Korver in 2017, it wasn't easy for the three-point shooter to leave Atlanta, a city he loved and a place where he had spent five seasons. But, thanks to his likeable personality and consistent play on the court, Korver fit in very well. He has called the Cavs locker room "amazing" and even convinced former teammate Deron Williams to sign with Cleveland. Korver's dream, of course, is that ever-elusive championship ring. Therefore, teaming up with King James, who wears three of them, is a no-brainer.

BIG ASSIST | Aside from having a sweet shot, Korver's a pretty sweet guy: after winning the 2014–15 NBA Sportsmanship Award, he donated the $10,000 prize to the Helping Hand Charity Mission.

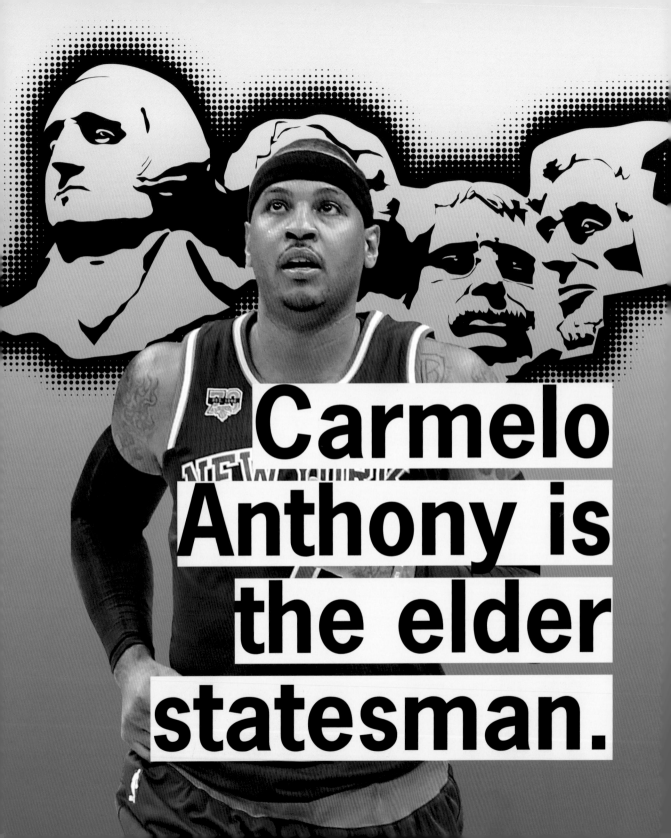

Carmelo Anthony is the elder statesman.

Carmelo Anthony
New York Knicks
Small Forward

Carmelo Anthony has entered a new phase of his career. Melo was the young, confident face of the Denver Nuggets when he entered the league as the third-overall pick in 2003. Now he's a seasoned veteran for his hometown New York Knicks and one of the biggest names in the game.

He's the face of the Knicks franchise who stayed true to New York by playing through a team rebuild. The franchise now shows promise after the addition of Derrick Rose and Joakim Noah, both from the Chicago Bulls, and the drafting of 7-foot-3 Kristaps Porzingis.

Melo sees a bright future for Porzingis. "He's going to lead this organization long after I'm retired," he said to sbnation.com in 2016, and the site has started calling this older and wiser version of Anthony "Dad Melo." His play on the court attests to this change in nickname. He no longer feels the need to do it all himself. He doesn't hog the ball, and his new habit of passing the rock nearly had him score a triple-double in early January 2016.

The 6-foot-8, 240-pound small forward is one of the most versatile in the game, and while he can shift to power forward, he's best at the three spot, where he can post up, step back or take over a game with lights-out shooting. Watch out, when he gets hot he's nearly unstoppable. He dropped 62 points on the Madison Square Garden floor in 2014 — which broke Knicks legend Bernard King's record — and he is still the same player who led the league in scoring 2012–13. With nine

7

NBA All-Star nods and gold medals at the 2008, 2012 and 2016 Olympics, New York fans hope Dad can bring them a championship.

Beyond the court, Melo's all about giving back. He took 250 kids to see the *Alvin and the Chipmunks* movie in 2015. His foundation also raises money for school supplies, and his businesses stretch from fashion to technology to owning a soccer team. (Seriously. He owns Puerto Rico FC.) He even released a line of products called *Turtles by Melo*, based on the Teenage Mutant Ninja Turtles, and he had a cameo in the 2016 movie!

Melo's still got it, and although he's transitioning from superstar to mentor, the past several seasons proved his game is adaptable. If he keeps passing the ball, running the floor and scoring at will, his career will go down as one of the best in the modern era.

HE'S ON FIRE!

On Melo's 62-point night, he hit 23 of 35 shots, drained a half-court shot at the buzzer before halftime and didn't even play the whole game!

Dwight Howard
Charlotte Hornets
Center

8

Dwight Howard sometimes comes off as a giant kid with a goofy grin. But far from immature, he's one of the most giving athletes in the sport and a model for how basketball players can help their communities. He's also a behemoth on the boards, with his 7-foot, 4½-inch wingspan, and one of the best defensive players in the league.

Howard was a phenom growing up in Atlanta, Georgia, who dominated the high school landscape, and led his team to a state championship with 25 points and 18 rebounds per game during his senior season. He was one of the last players to jump straight from high school to the NBA. Howard — now topping out at 6-foot-11 and 265 pounds — was taken number one by the Orlando Magic in 2004.

Howard's a dependable double-double factory, and he eventually led the Magic all the way to the NBA final in 2008–09, knocking off LeBron James and the Cleveland Cavaliers in the Eastern Conference final then losing to the Kobe Bryant–led LA Lakers. Howard racked up awards during this time, including Defensive Player of the Year three years in a row.

The freakishly athletic Howard — his vertical leap is 39½ inches and his vertical reach is 12 feet, 6 inches — also led the NBA in rebounds five times and blocks twice. And everyone remembers his superhero moment from the 2007 Dunk Contest: not only was he decked out in a cape and Superman T-shirt, he leapt in the air and slammed the ball from several feet above the rim for a perfect 10.

The eight-time All-Star has had some rough spots in his career. Over the last five seasons he's bounced around the league, with stops in Los Angeles, Houston and Atlanta. In June 2017 Howard was traded to the Charlotte Hornets, where he could be the piece Charlotte needs to move up in the Eastern Conference.

In his personal life, Howard's faith has led him to be extremely active in charities, including literacy programs. While in Orlando he regularly took kids from the Boys and Girls Club shopping for shoes and spent time at local hospitals. A former Orlando Magic GM said no one had done as much as Howard to better the community. That carried over to Houston, where he ran basketball camps and anti-bullying campaigns through his D12 Foundation. He's proving one day at a time that Superman may just be a regular guy after all.

KRYPTONITE! Howard's super powers don't extend to the free-throw line. Over the course of his career, he's rarely reached the 60% mark.

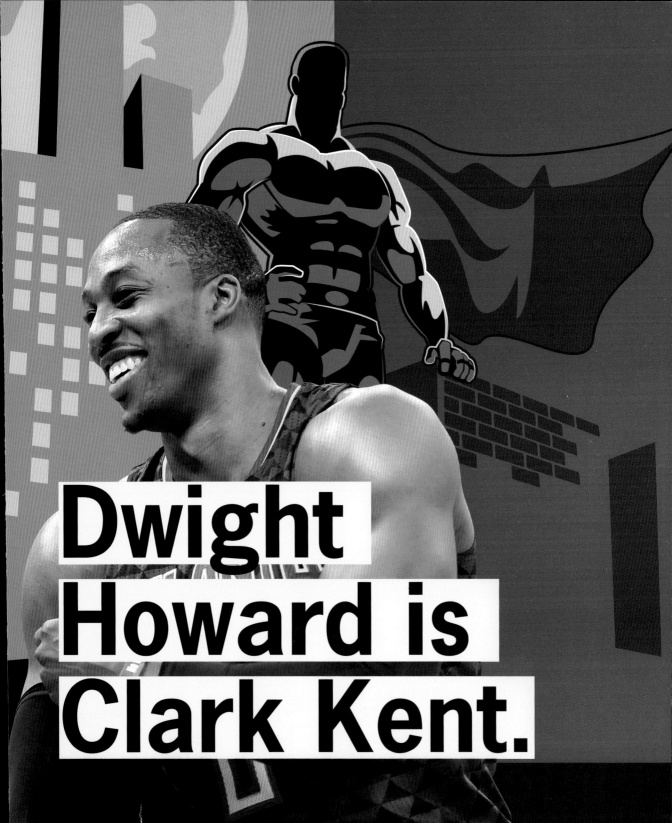

Dwight Howard is Clark Kent.

Klay Thompson
Golden State Warriors Shooting Guard

11

Expectations might crush you when you're the son of a former number-one pick. Not so for Klay Thompson. As the quieter half of the Golden State Warriors' "Splash Brothers," he's making his mark as a premiere perimeter shooter who's part of one of the greatest duos the NBA has ever seen.

Thompson is a West Coast product through and through. He grew up in Oregon, where he played high school ball with future NBA star Kevin Love and where his father, Mychal, played with the Portland Trail Blazers. His father also played with the LA Lakers, winning two titles late in his career. Now the younger Thompson, who was drafted 11th overall in 2011 by the Warriors, is molding a stellar career in the Bay Area, having already secured two titles of his own.

In 2015–16 he set a career high with 22.1 points per game and a 47% field-goal percentage. Golden State may have lost the NBA title that year to the Cleveland Cavaliers, but Klay put his stamp on the playoffs with an unforgettable performance in Game 6 of the Western Conference final versus the Oklahoma City Thunder. In that game, Thompson finished with 41 points and a playoff-record 11 threes!

It wasn't the first time Thompson had thrilled fans with a hot streak: January 23, 2015, will go down in history as one of the most incredible shooting performances fans have ever seen. Klay went crazy, scoring an NBA record 37 points in the third quarter on 13-of-13 shooting, including nine threes. No one else has ever been that hot over 12 minutes. He finished with a cool 52 that night. And that's the thing: Thompson is as cool as they come, a laid-back but lethal shooter who destroys defenders who, night after night, refuse to respect his shot.

Thompson knocked off Splash Brother Steph Curry in the 2016 Three-Point Contest, which added fuel to the fire over who is truly the best shooter in the league. And if three-point shots aren't your thing, Thompson plays well on the other side of the ball too, playing tight defense and rarely giving uncontested looks.

It seems the sky's the limit with Thompson, who is under contract for several more years with the Warriors. With the addition of Kevin Durant in 2016, Golden State has three of the best shooters in the NBA on the court at the same time! But perhaps the best one of all is the quietest one, lurking in the shadows, swinging off a screen and dropping another dagger into the hearts of his opponents.

SCULPTING THE NEXT GEN

Klay is super active in the community, and together with his father and the Currys, he hosts the annual Splash Brothers Clinic, a day-long basketball camp that raises money for the Warriors Community Foundation.

Klay Thompson always makes a splash.

×29

Isaiah Thomas is on another level.

Isaiah Thomas
Boston Celtics
Point Guard

When you're one of the smallest players in the NBA, you spend a lot of time looking up at your opponents. For 5-foot-9 Isaiah Thomas, the 2016–17 season has been the first time in his career he's been able to look down on the pack — as one of the NBA's top scorers.

It hasn't been an easy journey for the pint-sized point guard. Thomas got his start in college with the Washington Huskies, the alma mater of Nate Robinson, another short NBA star. Thomas played three years for the Huskies, but his size prevented scouts from seeing his full potential. He was drafted 60th overall in 2011 by the Sacramento Kings. Thomas lasted three seasons as point guard in the California capital, and during the 2014 off-season he was sent packing to the Phoenix Suns. He dressed for just 46 games due to an excess of other guards and an injury. But from Phoenix Thomas landed in Boston, where he has thrived. The break he needed came in the 2015–16 season, when he was named starting point guard for the Boston Celtics.

Thomas started smashing records during the 2016–17 season, and everyone around the league took notice. He dropped 52 points against the Miami Heat, including 29 in the fourth quarter, a new Celtics mark of excellence that eclipsed Boston legend Larry Bird. Thomas also scored 20 points or more in 41 straight games, which bested Celtics great John Havlicek. His clutch fourth quarter shooting and season average of 29 points have earned him

league-wide praise, and in close games, it's you-know-who who's getting the ball for the final shot.

What makes someone of his size so good? Fearlessness, for one. Thomas isn't afraid to drive to the basket, using stutter-step moves, hesitation and gusto to maneuver toward the hoop. Celtics coach Brad Stevens said of Thomas at the end of the 2015–16 season, "He's not afraid of conflict or confrontation and at the same time he's going to put his arm around you. He's got a nice balance in that regard."

If you're wondering whether Thomas was named after Detroit Pistons point guard and Hall of Famer Isiah Thomas, he was! The year Isaiah was born, his dad, an LA Lakers fan, lost a bet to a friend who was a Pistons fan.

No one would have predicted this 5-foot-9 guard drafted 60th overall would make it to the top of the pile. Now a two-time All-Star and one of the league's top scorers, Thomas has quickly risen up the ranks of the NBA.

Good things come in small packages, as the saying goes, and it seems like Thomas plans on delivering for years to come.

HELPING KIDS BOUNCE BACK

Thomas is definitely one to give back. In early 2017 he opened the Isaiah Thomas Court at the Boys and Girls Club in his hometown, Tacoma, Washington. The point guard was also awarded an NBA Community Assist Award in December 2016.

Dirk Nowitzki
Dallas Mavericks
Power Forward

41

Dirk Nowitzki is one of the greatest international stars the game has ever produced. The German center has been a dominant force for nearly 20 years, thanks in part to an incredible step-back jumper, unselfish play and a personality that shines through every time he steps on the court.

Nowitzki was drafted ninth overall and acquired by the Dallas Mavericks in a draft-day swap in 1998. He entered the Mavs' lineup for the 1998–99 season with little fanfare, but the following season, he began turning heads by averaging 17.5 points per game. By 2006–07 the center, who had ushered in a new and impressive era of European NBA stars, became the first Euro to ever be named league MVP. That season he went 50.2% from the field and averaged 24.6 points, 8.9 rebounds and 3.4 assists as Dallas notched 67 wins. He also put up one of the few 50-40-90 seasons (50% from the field, 40% from behind the arc and 90% from the free-throw line) — impressive for a seven footer!

But the Mavs were taken out in the first round of the playoffs that year despite being overwhelming favorites, and Nowitzki took the brunt of the criticism. That's why in 2011, when the Mavericks won the NBA final, it was sweet revenge for a player who many saw as unable to win a championship. It was a lesson in persevering through tough times, and it finally cemented his reputation as one of the game's greats. Now, as he nears the end of his career, he's already in the top ten of all-time scoring. And many of those points have come courtesy of his go-to move, the patented pick-and-pop that leaves defenses mesmerized.

Current Golden State Warriors coach Steve Kerr said in 2014, "He leaves you shaking your head every time. It's remarkable."

Do you switch or stay with the man? Dirk's kept defenders guessing his entire career, stepping back for a three or putting the ball on the floor and going to the hoop. And if he gets fouled, he's near perfect from the line. Even playing fewer minutes per contest in 2015–16, he still put up 18.3 points per game while shooting nearly 90% from the line and 38% from distance.

The big man has been an even larger pillar in the Dallas community and abroad, hosting charity baseball and soccer tournaments through his foundation. The NBA has recognized his achievements helping kids. His good buddy and former teammate Steve Nash put it this way: "I don't know if there's ever been anybody like Dirk."

There might not be a better way to sum up his career.

EXCLUSIVE CLUB | Nowitzki is the only player in NBA history to register 25,000 points, 10,000 rebounds, 1,000 blocks and 1,000 three-pointers!

Dirk
Nowitzki is
Mr. Efficient.

Kyrie Irving fears nothing.

Kyrie Irving
Cleveland Cavaliers Point Guard

There's a good chance many of you knew the smooth moves of Kyrie Irving before he was with the Cleveland Cavaliers. Do you remember those Pepsi Max ads with crazy Uncle Drew? Maybe you've YouTubed them since they aired in 2012. Well, high-flying old Uncle Drew is really Kyrie Irving. And did you ever watch the Disney series *Kickin' It*? Yup, that's Irving too. He was just a rookie in his first NBA season then. Now the point guard is an NBA superstar with a flair for the dramatic and one thought on his mind: establishing his legacy as one of the greatest point guards of his generation.

Irving's father, also a basketball pro, was playing in Australia when Kyrie was born, so he's both an American and an Australian citizen. However, the point guard honed his skills in New Jersey, where he dominated the local scene as a teenager before landing at Duke, one of the best colleges in the country. He was too good to stay long, though, and Cleveland made him the number-one overall pick in the 2011 NBA draft.

Now he's a household name. He was the 2014 All-Star Game MVP, and when the Cavaliers won the NBA championship in 2015–16, it was Irving who hit the go-ahead basket to beat the Golden State Warriors in a thrilling seven-game series. This moment was especially poignant considering Irving had missed the 2015 final with a knee injury. He then capped off his banner year with a gold medal at the Rio Olympics.

Irving's not the biggest point guard — 6-foot-3 and 193 pounds — but he's lightning quick off the dribble and his crossover has "shimmy shake" written all over it. He scored over 50 points twice during the 2014–15 season. Those are dominating numbers.

Two things make Irving really good: his willingness to drive to the basket and his killer shot. He's averaged a tidy 21.6 points, 5.8 assists and 3.4 rebounds over his career, and ever since he arrived in Cleveland, he's been the heart and soul of the team. He's also got a big heart off the court: in 2013 he lent a helping hand by visiting children in South Africa through UNICEF.

Although he's one of the NBA's true nice guys off the court, Irving's on-court persona is all about competitive fire, which fans in Cleveland are hoping will deliver many championships. The Cavs look like the team to beat in the East for years to come now that LeBron James has agreed to a long-term contract in Cleveland. And with Irving hungry for more and a confidence that knows no bounds — his Twitter handle sports the quote "fear is not real" — don't count the Cavs out as repeat champions.

COACH KYRIE

In 2016 Irving teamed up with Best Buddies, a charity that supports people with intellectual and developmental disabilities. Participants in the Basketball Challenge had a chance to play for a team coached by Irving.

Photo Credits